I0532219

Perfectly Imperfect

Unleashing Your Purpose Journal

Shaneé McCambry

Copyright © Shaneé McCambry

All rights reserved.

No portion of this book may be reproduced in any form without written permission from the publisher or author, except as permitted by U.S. copyright law. For permissions, bulk orders, and to inquire about speaking engagements, contact:

info@theperfectlyimperfectbook.com

Contents

Introduction

M any of us struggle with feeling inadequate. Many of us hesitate to take the plunge because we don't believe that we can rise to the occasion, or hesitate to promote ourselves because we don't think we deserve it. These feelings can hold us back in life and prevent us from achieving our dreams. I know something about that.

It's time to stop letting those feelings hold you back.

I'm Shaneé McCambry. Today I'm an author, business owner, and founder of the current Women That Win women's empowerment conference. But it took me a long time to feel that I was enough, or that I had the right to chase my dreams.

Once I began sharing my own darkest thoughts following a family tragedy, I was shocked by the response: so many people told me that they had felt the same way, but had believed that they were alone, or that their feelings of inadequacy really did mean that they were not enough. People said that hearing from someone in my position, that I'd been through the same thing helped them to feel less alone, and to believe in themselves.

This has become part of my mission: to help women everywhere to examine those things which make us feel less-than, and to see how owning our pain can make us *more* powerful, not less powerful. And that is what this journal is all about.

This journal is made to go with my memoir, "Perfectly Imperfect," which tells my own story in detail and invites the reader to reflect on their own life and where they can find power in the places that once made them feel weak. For maximum effect, I recommend that you go get that book as well so that you can see the experiences I discuss.

There we will discuss major life traumas like sexual assault and medical trauma, to the powerful impact of seemingly "minor" invalidating conversations which teach us not to trust ourselves or our abilities. We will see how these can negatively influence our mental health—and how we can unlearn the teachings that may be holding us back.

If you are using this journal alone, you can still benefit from the questions it asks.

You can repeat these exercises with different life events as often as you need. I do encourage you to find a real-life community of people you trust to do these exercises with. It may be helpful to find a community of people who have experienced and overcome what you've experienced. The power of speaking your truth out loud, and being seen and validated, is transformative for all involved.

I am also a huge advocate for therapy, and I highly recommend finding a therapist who you connect with and trust. Therapy has helped me tremendously on my journey, as you will soon learn. It's not just for "bad" moments in our lives.

Finally, I ask you to take your time, give yourself space for honesty and vulnerability, and take care of yourself as you take the brave steps to dig into your personal traumas and heal.

Chapter One

Second Time's the Charm, Right?

The first chapter of my memoir begins with this chapter title. It discusses my second suicide attempt. I wanted to start there because I wanted readers to understand that, no matter how low you are feeling—even if you have been feeling low for a very long time—you are not alone. And it's not too late.

I hit rock bottom and tried to kill myself *twice* before I was fortunate enough to find the people I could learn from, who would teach me to protect my peace and control my destiny. Now I hope to pay forward the generosity of those people, and the good fortune which brought them into my life at crucial times, by sharing all that I can with those who may be in the same place I was in years ago.

As we begin this book, I want us to focus on what we want to achieve. It's difficult to end up where you want to be if you don't know where that is. So I encourage you now to dream big, not paying attention to what feels possible or "reasonable" to you. This book is all about expanding your self-belief and your abilities, so start with your dream life.

What are your dreams, goals, and desires? Dream BIG—whatever you dream, I promise there is a series of steps you can take to achieve it if you want to. And in this book, we will focus on giving you the confidence to start undertaking those steps.

Throughout this book, I will invite you to journal deeply on one question each day. This will give your brain and body the time to deeply consider these questions, and grow and change around the answers you find.

Week 1, Day 1

What is the ideal career, relationship, or lifestyle you desire? Describe as many of these desires as you like, and stop when it feels overwhelming.

In my perfect life, I want:

_____

_____

_____

_____

_____

_____

_____

_____

_____

_____

Week 1, Day 2

Today, I invite you to read over what you wrote yesterday. How does it feel? Is there any part of you that feels bad or frightened for asking for such big things? Do you feel excited by the possibilities? Do you feel *both* things?

Try to fill a whole page with your thoughts and feelings. Your feelings are important, and they warrant being written down and studied, even if you are not sure what to write. Stop when you feel exhausted.

When I think of my dreams, I feel:

_____

_____

_____

_____

_____

_____

_____

_____

_____

_____

_____

_____

_____

_____

_____

_____

_____

_____

_____

Week 1, Day 3

Today, I invite you to read over what you wrote the last two days. How does that feel? If you feel guilty or ashamed of your desires, or if you feel you dreamed too big, do you think you are being fair to yourself? We are often harder on ourselves than we ever would be on other people.

What would you say to another woman if she expressed the same feelings to you? Would you say that she deserves to have what she wants? Would you encourage her that she deserves these things and is capable of having them?

If I met myself on the street, I would tell myself:

_____

_____

_____

_____

_____

_____

_____

_____

Week 1, Day 4

Read over your last several days of writing. How do you feel about accomplishing your dreams now? What do you think is needed for you to accomplish your dreams? Is it an internal sense of deservingness? A sense of your own competence? Or do you feel ready and eager to go, but you may need some specific knowledge about business, finance, relationships, your chosen craft, or something else in order to begin meeting the concrete milestones that will get you there?

To reach my dreams, I need:

_____

_____

_____

_____

_____

_____

_____

_____

Week 1, Day 5

In addition to our desires, it is important that we live in accordance with our values. If we are not clear on what our values and principles are, and what kind of difference we feel called to make in the world, we may end up feeling unsatisfied even if we get everything we thought we wanted.

What are your core values? Identifying your core values sets the foundation for your expectations. What are the principles that guide your life? What matters most to you? What kind of difference do you want to create in the world?

_____

_____

_____

_____

_____

_____

_____

_____

Week 1, Day 6

Read over your previous days' writings. You're a pretty impressive person, huh? What do you think of yourself now that you see your dreams, desires, feelings, and values laid out on paper?

Psychologists say that we fall in love with people when we learn intimately about their desires and their pain. When we fall in love with someone, we want to take care of them, protect them, and advocate for them. We want to help them achieve their goals. I invite you now, and give you permission, to fall in love with yourself.

How do you feel about yourself now, after reading your own intimate thoughts and feelings? How would you like to take care of yourself moving forward?

_____

_____

_____

_____

_____

_____

_____

Week 1, Day 7
Day of Rest

Today, rest and reflect on what you have learned over the previous days this week.

Take time to treat yourself to something you enjoy.

Chapter Two

Shhh...Our Little Secret...

A big part of my journey has been bringing the things I was taught to be ashamed of into the light. Too often in our society, victims are made to feel at fault for the harm that is done to them. They are told that there must be something wrong with *them* for this to happen to them, or that it must be in some way their fault.

This is true for traumas ranging from assault to less physical forms of bullying and mistreatment. Almost all of us likely have some sort of pain in our past, whether it is a major childhood trauma or one or more relationships in which we were told that we were incompetent or that we couldn't trust our own judgment. Prepare yourself now for some heavy lifting.

As a child, I was molested from the ages of four to eight years old. I was told that I mustn't tell, or I would also be in trouble. I was made to feel guilty if I didn't accept my abuser's treatment of me, or even support him in it. I was told that I didn't have the right to have needs, feelings, or boundaries, and that I was causing trouble if I didn't simply agree to how others chose to treat me.

When my abuser was caught by my family, much of the blame quickly shifted to me. Why hadn't I done more to stop the assaults on me? How could I now ask the family to ruin this promising young man's life by going to the police?

I was expected to suppress my own feelings and trauma and act like the attack never happened. If I spoke up about it, then I was the one who was deemed to be causing problems.

This is true of too many victims of all manner of assault and abuse. Society often feels that it is easiest to pretend that bad things never happened, and disregards any damage that isn't visible, such as damage to our sense of our own autonomy and worth. If not addressed adequately, these senses that we do not deserve autonomy or protection can carry through into our adult lives and lead us to accept unacceptable treatment from others, and to blame ourselves for things that aren't our fault.

If you are ready, let's address these traumas now. Let's address any feelings of being violated, any feelings that we don't deserve to have needs or autonomy. Let's drag the things we have been asked not to face out into the light, so that we can face them together and reframe them.

After all, our traumas are not our failings. They are evidence of our strength as survivors.

This week we are going to journal about times we may have felt shamed into silence, and view these events as though they were happening to someone else. We will ask if we have been fair to ourselves, and consider how we can be more fair to ourselves in the future.

Week 2, Day 1

What was something that happened to you when you were little that you haven't felt you could talk about? Why did you feel that way? Was it because you felt it was "your fault," or because you felt the harm done to you "wasn't important?"

_____

_____

_____

_____

_____

_____

_____

_____

_____

_____

What would you say to a stranger if you learned that they had experienced the same thing? What would you want them to know? What kind of support would you tell them they deserve?

_____

_____

_____

_____

_____

_____

_____

_____

_____

_____

If it feels safe and comfortable, I invite you to imagine going back in time and telling this to your younger self.

Week 2, Day 2

We've already done some heavy lifting, huh? Today I invite you to go back and read over everything you wrote yesterday. How do you feel, seeing your own story through a fresh set of eyes? How do you think this might change your feelings moving forward?

_____

_____

_____

_____

_____

_____

_____

_____

_____

_____

_____

_____

_____

_____

_____

_____

_____

_____

_____

_____

_____

Week 2, Day 3

For the traumatic event you wrote about on Day 1, how do you think this event changed you? Is there a fear you developed because of it? Is there something you don't do anymore, or are afraid to try, because of it?

_____

_____

_____

_____

_____

_____

_____

_____

_____

_____

_____

_____

_____

_____

_____

_____

_____

_____

_____

_____

_____

_____

_____

_____

Have these fears or changes interfered with you meeting your goals, or obtaining your desires? If so, do you feel more empowered to do these things you may have given up now that you have viewed what happened to you through a new lens? What do you think it would take to remove this obstacle from your path?

_____

_____

_____

_____

_____

_____

_____

_____

_____

_____

Week 2, Day 4

Too often our society places responsibility for wrongs on the victim. Sometimes this is because adults and authority figures simply are not sure what the best way to respond is, and they have not prioritized learning.

For your trauma, how do you wish your family, or the other adults involved, had handled this situation? What would you have asked them to do if you felt you were allowed to ask for what you needed?

_____

_____

_____

_____

_____

_____

_____

_____

What kind of support would you give to someone if you found out they were experiencing a trauma like your own today? Are you able to give this kind of support to yourself right now?

_____

_____

_____

_____

_____

_____

_____

_____

_____

_____

_____

Week 2, Day 5

One way we can help to heal our own traumas is to make the world a safer and more supportive place for others in the future.

What do you want to tell the world about what happened to you? What do you want people to know about how it affected you, and how you wish they would handle it if something similar happens to someone in their life?

_____

_____

_____

_____

_____

_____

_____

_____

_____

_____

Week 2, Day 6

We have done some heavy lifting, remembering times when we may not have felt powerful in our lives.

In a perfect world, we can bring compassion and healing to ourselves, now that we are able to see how deserving we really are. We can come away feeling empowered, realizing that we did not deserve what happened to us and that we have shown our strength by all we have accomplished and all the ways we have continued to grow and thrive since our trauma. But since we have spent so much time in that space

Today, I invite you to read back over everything you wrote down for Weeks 1 and 2. Take this as a reminder of what a strong and fascinating person you are, and how much support you deserve.

How do you feel now that you have read over what you have written for Week 1 and Week 2? Did you learn anything, or did you find that any feelings, goals, or desires have shifted?

_____

_____

_____

_____

_____

Week 2, Day 7

Today I invite you to make a list of accomplishments you are proud of. These can be things you have done that are measurable from the outside, or they can be internal things you are proud of such as your attitude, your passions, and your kindness toward others.

Since we often do not give ourselves enough credit for the things we do and the wonderful things about ourselves, I am going to go ahead and *require* you to find ten things you are proud of about yourself and list them here. If you have trouble, consider that it might not be that there is nothing to be proud of—it is far more likely that you are not giving yourself enough credit. Consider this to be your *assignment* to give yourself credit.

I am proud of:

1. _____

2. _____

3. _____

4. _____

5. _____

6. _____

7. _____

8. _____

9. _____

10. _____

Chapter Three

The Rollercoaster of Emotions

When I was a teenager, I had a breast cancer scare. Around the same time, I was told that, according to my gynecologists' findings, I may be unable to have children of my own.

That's a lot for a teenager to handle, right? And I now realize it was made worse by the culture of silence that prevailed in my life. Many of the adults around me did not know how to hold space for a child's emotions, or know how to support them.

This was common in our parents' generation. Especially in the Black and Brown communities, there may have been an element of self-preservation. There were times when it was physically dangerous for our ancestors to express their true feelings, or seek justice for abuses.

In some cases this has carried over into a culture in which discipline means silence, and adults think that the best way for them to prepare children to succeed as adults is to teach them to keep quiet about their true feelings. This can teach children not to trust their feelings, and, in my case, not to trust even my own body.

One extension of our society's tendency to victim blame can also be a sense of shame about medical issues. One need not look far on the Internet or in certain health and wellness circles to find the attitude that if someone is sick, it must be because they did something wrong. For too many people, this can result in concealing medical issues or feeling ashamed or frightened to seek treatment.

This is similar to the attitude of blaming people for traumas they suffered at the hands of other people, or as a result of forces beyond their control. Because it is uncomfortable to think about illness, some people in our society blame victims of illness for contracting it and pressure them to keep quiet about their conditions in public.

Fortunately, around the time of my health scares, I also had some places in my life where I felt powerful and essential. Through sports at school and through my local African American history museum, I received the message that I was able to excel and do work that was important to me and to other people.

Sports even gave me some degree of confidence in my body, even though at some level I felt that my reproductive organs had betrayed me, and that this may have been because of the years I spent enduring sexual assaults.

I truly believe that these outlets prevented me from retreating into myself entirely while I was going through these isolating experiences which those around me did not know how to support me in. Activities where we feel essential, strong, or powerful can transform the way we approach all aspects of our life.

In this chapter we will talk about our confidence in ourselves. Where do we feel powerful, essential, or useful? How can we carry these feelings with us into life to become more effective at pursuing our goals and principles, and advocating for ourselves and others?

Week 3, Day 1

As always, we will start with identifying possible challenges, and then move on to pursuing solutions.

How do you feel about your body? Do you see it as an ally or an enemy? Why do you think that is?

_____

_____

_____

_____

_____

_____

_____

_____

_____

Do you think that your feelings about your body affect your sense of your own competence, usefulness, or power? Do you think there is a connection between how you feel about your worthiness or ability to change the world and how you feel about your body? How would changing those feelings about your body help you reach your goals?

_____

_____

_____

_____

_____

_____

_____

_____

_____

_____

Week 3, Day 2

Who or what do you think shaped the way you feel about your body? Try not to focus on your body's abilities or health status, since people with similar disabilities and medical conditions can feel very different about themselves and their bodies. Instead, try focusing on the messages that the culture and the people around you have sent you about your body. These might include events where people treated you a certain way about your health or your physical abilities, messages about how a person's body, or your body in particular, "should" be, etc..

_____

_____

_____

_____

_____

_____

_____

_____

Now, I invite you to look over what you have written in the past two days. Do these judgments about your body and your health seem fair to you? What would you say to someone who told you they felt this way?

_____

_____

_____

_____

_____

_____

_____

_____

_____

_____

_____

_____

Week 3, Day 3

Even though many of us come into adulthood with some negative feelings about our bodies and our abilities, there are many ways in which we can learn through experience that we are strong and competent.

Where in your life do you feel essential? Is there a group, place, or role where you feel you are doing important work? If you can't think of such a place, what might your ideal role be? What kind of team would you like to be an essential part of?

_____

_____

_____

_____

_____

_____

_____

_____

_____

Whether or not you already have an answer for the question above, what kind of work would feel useful, essential, and meaningful to you? Is there an issue you'd like to take action on, or a problem you'd like to solve? How might you find groups that might be able to help you do this work?

_____

_____

_____

_____

_____

_____

_____

_____

_____

Week 3, Day 4

Where do you feel physically powerful? Are there any activities you engage in that allow you to test and marvel at your body's capabilities? How do you feel after you complete these activities? If you are disabled or suffer from poor health, do not assume that this feeling is out of reach for you. I have been privileged in my time to be acquainted with a number of actors, dancers, and essential production staff with disabilities, and on one memorable occasion a wheelchair basketball league. These questions are not made only for able-bodied and healthy people.

_____

_____

_____

_____

_____

_____

_____

_____

If you don't have anything in your life that makes you feel physically powerful, what would you like to try that could accomplish that? Do you feel drawn to martial arts or acrobatics? How about dance or yoga? If you are concerned that your health may stop you from participating in these activities, is there a teacher you can consult who may be able to teach you a different version? What sport or art do you love enough that it might coax you to become physically powerful and confident? If you have an activity you already engage in which gives you this feeling, are there ways you can further incorporate those feelings to your daily life?

_____

_____

_____

_____

_____

_____

_____

_____

I encourage you once again to discuss the answers to these questions with your support group. You might be surprised and inspired to hear how the people around you answer these questions. You might inspire someone else by talking about your own experiences!

As we dig deeper and begin to value ourselves more, we radiate that power outward. We can inspire others to do the same. When we value our own work and see how others value our work, we understand what ordinary people just like us can accomplish by God's grace.

Let us step out of the shadows and into the light, embracing the power within. Let us remember that we are worthy of this happy moment, of this success, and being our perfectly imperfect selves.

Week 3, Days 5-7
Days of Rest

On these days, I invite you to take a break from self-reflection. Instead, consider engaging in something that makes you feel powerful or useful. If you are considering taking up a new physical hobby or a new kind of purpose-driven work, you may use these days to research these endeavors and take steps to get started in them!

Chapter Four

Let Your Light Shine

I n high school, I received quite a few honors. In part, this was *because* of my trauma. My sense of inadequacy drove me to push myself very hard to prove myself adequate, and my own experiences gave me compassion and kindness stemming from the knowledge that everyone is fighting their own invisible battle. As a result, I was chosen for a prestigious cheerleading engagement and elected Homecoming Queen by my classmates.

This created an interesting situation. Although I had achievements, between the trauma that helped drive me to work so hard and the messages I was still getting that it was wrong for me to be too proud of my achievements, I did not *feel* as accomplished and popular as I probably looked on the outside. In fact, just two short years later I would make my first suicide attempt after feeling I had disappointed everyone's high expectations of me.

In time, I began to notice a common pattern in the communities I grew up in: men who were confident and proud of their achievements were viewed as cool and smooth, confident and competent; but women and children were treated as "prideful" and "arrogant" when we displayed the same satisfaction with our own work. It has taken me a long time to unlearn that patriarchal attitude.

I know what it is to have done something remarkable—yet be unable to *feel* that accomplishment in your bones and give yourself sufficient credit for it. So I want us to spend this week giving ourselves credit for our remarkable accomplishments and examining if we really give ourselves enough credit for our work.

Week 4, Day 1

What is a victory you have had *today*? This can be a small thing, but extra points if you've done something that you've struggled to accomplish in the past. How were you able to accomplish this victory?

_____

_____

_____

_____

_____

_____

_____

_____

_____

_____

Week 4, Day 2

What do you think is the biggest battle you ever won in your life? Do you think your past self gave herself enough credit for that achievement? What would you say if you could visit that past version of yourself now?

_____

_____

_____

_____

_____

_____

_____

_____

_____

_____

_____

_____

_____

_____

_____

_____

_____

_____

_____

_____

_____

_____

Week 4, Day 3

When you think about taking pride in your work, or giving yourself credit for your victories, what does that feel like in your body? How does it feel in your body to know that you are strong and competent, or to know that you have succeeded? Write the physical sensations out in as much detail as you can.

_____

_____

_____

_____

_____

_____

_____

_____

_____

Take a long moment to recall and imagine the feeling of success in your body now. Can you create this feeling in your body by focusing on these sensations?

_____

_____

_____

_____

_____

_____

_____

_____

_____

Week 4, Day 4

What victories would you like to achieve in your future? What would you like to accomplish that you have had a hard time seeing as realistic? Do they still feel so unrealistic, now that you've visited your past victories?

_____

_____

_____

_____

_____

_____

_____

_____

_____

_____

Week 4, Day 5

Completing this journal is in itself a big victory. It means you are taking time to devote to caring for yourself, and empowering yourself to take the next steps on your journey. It's often difficult to make time, so this is a big deal!

What does completing this journal mean to you? What has motivated you to achieve this victory?

_____

_____

_____

_____

_____

_____

_____

_____

_____

Week 4, Days 6 & 7
Days of Rest

You have done a lot of work already! Take a breather.

Take the time to do something nice for yourself on these days. You may also wish to read over your answers to some past questions and reflect on them, if you would like to keep the inner work going.

Chapter Five

A New Beginning

College was at once one of the most difficult and one of the most powerful times in my life. I was meeting people who were raised with very different ways of thinking from my own community's, and I was lucky enough to learn a lot from them.

Yet at the same time, I felt incredibly isolated and inadequate. I left high school with sky-high expectations on my shoulders due to my top tier performance my senior year. Due to an administrative error, I found myself attending my second choice school instead of my first choice.

To make matters worse, I was asked to make a deal in order to secure my housing at my new school. In order for my stepdad to pay for my housing, I was asked to call my dad up and say a bunch of things I didn't want to say about how he had let me down as a father. I couldn't finance my housing on my own; even worse, I felt I would be causing problems for my mother and the family unit if I said "no" to my stepdad.

As I walked the campus grounds, I thought everyone else seemed more confident and at ease than me. I felt like an imposter. My rift with my father festered inside me. I felt like a failure as a daughter: I could not please my dad and my stepdad both at once, no matter what I did.

This sensation of a double-bind was pervasive in my life because of the expectations I'd been raised with. Growing up, I internalized the idea that making everyone happy was my responsibility, even if it meant neglecting myself. Setting boundaries felt selfish, like I was betraying the "good girl" image people expected. But I could no longer even try to please everyone: the countless contradictory expectations people around me had of women in general, and me in particular, had become too much.

All of this isolation from my friends, conflict within my family, and financial difficulties led to my first suicide attempt my freshman year of college.

One of the most powerful things I learned from my college friends was the art of saying "no" with ease and grace. In the culture I was raised in, saying "no" was viewed as offensive. I was expected to be helpful and agreeable, and if I refused a request or voiced a dissenting opinion it was seen as disrespectful, a direct attack on or condemnation of the other person.

In the families of the friends I met at college, I saw different dynamics. I saw peers who were able to say "no, I won't do that, that's not who I am" and not be treated as though they were being hurtful or causing problems. I saw families where even children were allowed to say "no" and voice their honest feelings and opinions, and this did not cause a breakdown of discipline.

I did my best to learn from these peers and their families how I could be a strong, independent woman without feeling that I was being a "mean girl," and how I could let people get close to me while still retaining my ability to say "no" to them and assert my own boundaries. For the first time, I began to feel that there might be virtue in being true to myself and my own feelings, instead of viewing this as a selfish and harmful thing to do.

In this chapter, I want to talk about society's expectations of women, and people's expectations of you. I want to look at how you measure your success, and investigate the ways in which protecting your peace and filling your own cup affects your ability to meet your goals.

Week 5, Day 1

Society tells us to measure our success as women in certain ways, especially when we're young. What do you feel you must accomplish in order to be successful? When you think about these things you must accomplish to satisfy your own definition of success, do they feel fulfilling to you?

_____

_____

_____

_____

_____

_____

_____

_____

_____

_____

Week 5, Day 2

Who do you think decided how you measure your success? Whose expectations do you feel you have to meet, or who do you think taught you your ideas about what you must do in life?

_____

_____

_____

_____

_____

_____

_____

_____

_____

_____

Week 5, Day 3

How would you define success for yourself if there were no outside influences to please? What work would you most like to accomplish, or what would you most like to experience? Does that feel within reach right now, or is it similar to what you're already doing? How would it change your life if you pursued this work instead of other metrics of success?

_____

_____

_____

_____

_____

_____

_____

_____

Week 5, Day 4

What makes *you* happy? What are some things that will make you feel fulfilled? At peace? Take today just to meditate on these things, and how you feel in your body when you are doing or experiencing them.

_____

_____

_____

_____

_____

_____

_____

_____

_____

_____

Week 5, Day 5

What are some things that you are having a hard time saying "no" or "yes" to? What are some ways you think you can say "no" or "yes" so you can take control and put your own calling and well-being first?

_____

_____

_____

_____

_____

_____

_____

_____

_____

_____

Week 5, Day 6

Today, I invite you to read over what you have written on the previous days this week. Have your thoughts or feelings about how you want to spend your time, or what you want out of life, changed? Do you feel differently now than you did at the beginning of the week? If so, how?

_____

_____

_____

_____

_____

_____

_____

_____

_____

_____

Week 5, Day 7

Day of rest. Treat yourself to something nice. You deserve it.

Chapter Six

In the Darkness

Although I was seeing new possibilities for myself in college, I felt that I was all too often failing to achieve these. Financial problems mounted, as I was only able to work outside of school hours, and then my degree program began demanding that I be on-call for volunteer work outside of school hours as well.

At the same time, tensions continued mounting at home. On one occasion, I drove home for the holidays—only to be confronted by the sight of my abuser playing with my little cousin in the front yard.

Unsurprisingly, I lost it. I screamed at him to get away from her and began advancing toward him menacingly. In some ways, this was a breakthrough: I stood up for the little girl I had once been.

In other ways, it reinforced some of my trauma. Throughout the event, family members—most of whom had never been told about what happened to me by those who knew—looked at me like I was crazy. My abuser himself acted as though my reaction was unreasonable.

What I experienced on that visit home was called a trigger. "Trigger" comes from the simple idea of one thing that triggers another to occur. Some experiences can provoke almost uncontrollable reactions from us due to our past histories.

Triggers develop within the human mind as a survival reaction. When we believe we are being threatened, it makes sense to have a strong aggressive response. We saw one way in which such a response might be genuinely useful in the case of my abuser playing with the little girl.

Yet triggers can also be debilitating, if the reactions we have to them are not helpful to our situation. In these cases, it is useful to learn to manage the trigger, such as by removing yourself from situations where you know you might be triggered, or doing work to un-learn or change your triggered reaction.

I feel that there are also positive triggers. Some experiences and activities can remind us of good times in our lives, or remind us how far we've come. A negative trigger can even become a positive trigger if our changing responses can show us how far we've grown, healed, and evolved.

So when your triggers appear, don't get mad at the emotions they bring. We're designed to have emotions, and there's nothing shameful about that. The Bible tells us that Jesus displayed many emotions like anger, sadness, compassion, and irritation. He cried, and even flipped some tables.

Emotions are a part of being human that Jesus himself experienced. It's how we choose to respond to them that can make us great or not-so-great people to be around. We can choose to cultivate responses that are beneficial to ourselves and others, or we can blame other people for our emotions inappropriately and potentially cause trauma for them.

In this chapter we will talk about our triggers, and reflect on how we can work with them in the weeks ahead.

Week 6, Day 1

Think about the most recent experience that triggered some emotions like anger, sadness, fear, anxiety, etc. What happened just before you felt triggered? Was it a specific event, word, or interaction

_____

_____

_____

_____

_____

_____

_____

_____

_____

_____

How did you feel in your body before, during, and after the trigger? Did you experience any physical sensations like tightness, tingling, sweaty, shaky, or rapid heartbeat?

_____

_____

_____

_____

_____

_____

_____

_____

_____

_____

_____

What need might be underlying my triggered response? Do I need safety, validation, control, or something else?

_____

_____

_____

_____

_____

_____

_____

_____

_____

_____

Week 6, Day 2

Think about the times you have been angriest recently. What makes you angriest, and why? Are there any times you become angry that might seem disproportionate? Is there something you are being reminded of at these times?

_____

_____

_____

_____

_____

_____

_____

_____

_____

_____

Why do you think you might have such a strong anger response to those situations? Do you think that response is helpful, or unhelpful? The response might be helpful, like when you are triggered to actually defend someone who is in danger. Or it might be unhelpful, like when you become very angry with someone over a small mistake or difference of opinion. Some triggers may cause both reactions at different times. What about yours?

_____

_____

_____

_____

_____

_____

_____

_____

_____

_____

Triggering situations can be very stressful to us. Is there a way you can avoid triggering situations, or recognize that a triggering situation may be coming and remove yourself from the situation?

_____

_____

_____

_____

_____

_____

_____

_____

_____

_____

Week 6, Day 3

Triggering situations can be very challenging for us. And sometimes, challenges can help us learn and grow.

Is there a way you can use your triggering situations to grow and become more emotionally resilient? Can you use them as an opportunity to practice self-compassion, learn new coping skills, or seek support from a therapist?

_____

_____

_____

_____

_____

_____

_____

_____

_____

Week 6, Day 4

Today, spend some time with the affirmations below. These are affirmations I have learned, with the help of my therapist, to help me manage my triggers.Affirmations are declarations of faith or belief. They are positive statements that we say to ourselves as often as we need to to promote ideas that we want to have in the front of our minds. These can be ideas about ourselves which often promote well-being, self-belief, and personal growth.

Affirmations are typically "I am" or "I will" statements. After reading mine, choose some that you can connect with AND come up with a few of your own.

1. "My body is strong and capable of feeling and releasing."

2. "I am in control of my own thoughts and reactions."

3. "My past does not define me, it informs me."

4. "I forgive myself for my reactions and choose to learn from them."

5. "This trigger is an opportunity for growth and understanding."

6. "This trigger is helping me to identify my needs and build healthy boundaries."

7. "I trust in God's plan, even when I don't understand the path He has laid before me."

8. "I surrender my trigger to God, knowing I am not alone in my struggles."

Try saying each of the affirmations on the previous page out loud to yourself at least once. Try saying it slowly, clearly, and firmly, without shyness or hesitation. Try saying them outloud while looking at yourself directly in a mirror.

Once you have said each affirmation slowly and clearly aloud at least once, take a look at the questions on the following pages.

Choose your favorite affirmation from the list. When you say it aloud, slowly and clearly and confidently, how does that change the sensations in your body? How does it change your mindset?

_____

_____

_____

_____

_____

_____

_____

_____

Why do you think this affirmation might be your favorite? What does it speak to that your mind or body especially needs to hear?

_____

_____

_____

_____

_____

_____

_____

_____

_____

_____

_____

_____

Based on your answer to the last question, write a long and detailed affirmation for yourself. Most affirmations are short so we can recall them easily, but for this journaling exercise, I will ask you to write a whole page affirming the things you have discovered that your mind or body need to hear. This will allow you to dig deeper into what kinds of healing and growth your mind and body crave.

_____

_____

_____

_____

_____

_____

_____

_____

_____

Week 6, Day 5

Today, I invite you to read back over everything you have written this week. What have you learned about your triggers?

_____

_____

_____

_____

_____

_____

_____

_____

_____

_____

_____

Are there situations where your triggers serve you? Are there situations where they create distress or problems for you?

_____

_____

_____

_____

_____

_____

_____

_____

_____

_____

_____

_____

Which affirmations felt helpful to your mind and body? Do you think you will be able to use these in the future if you begin to feel triggered, or to experience another type of distress? In what sorts of situations might you be able to use the power of the changes these affirmations produce in your mind and body?

_____

_____

_____

_____

_____

_____

_____

_____

_____

_____

_____

Days 6 & 7

Days of Rest

Take these days to do something nice for yourself. If you like, you can take time to read back over your answers to the previous questions.

Chapter Seven

You Can Do It

My first failed suicide attempt motivated me to make changes in my life. There is nothing like hitting rock bottom to force a person out of their comfort zone. For me, that meant standing up for myself and my true feelings. It meant healing my relationship with my dad after the damage I'd done to it when I made that deal with my stepdad. It meant beginning to say "no" to things that I knew I simply couldn't do, where before I would have felt too afraid of causing offense or disappointing people's expectations. Many people are amazed by how much better life gets when they first begin enforcing their boundaries and expressing their true feelings and desires. While some people will respond badly, others will respond better than someone like me, who was taught that I wasn't allowed to say "no" or have needs, could ever expect. New views of possibility are opened once we start asking for what we really want.

One thing we can learn from this process is which relationships are keepers and which may not be. Some people will respond to our needs and boundaries with consistent hostility, trying to make us feel like we are a problem for having them. Others will respond supportively, encouraging us to take care of ourselves. Some people might move from the first category into the second as they adjust to the idea that you have needs and boundaries you didn't have before.The ones who don't move, well. They are not likely to be good allies on your life's journey.Recognizing that we can change our lives by asking for what we really want and expressing our true feelings is powerful. This means we can also make life better for future generations by creating new ways of raising children and supporting each other.

In the questions to come, we will examine how we wish to shape traditions. Traditions are ways of doing things that are passed down from generation to generation. These can be good, bad, or neutral. Some families may feel that their traditions are "the only way things can be," or "the way things have always been done." But once we begin to speak our truth, we can challenge these assumptions and ask how we can make life better for those who come after us.

Week 7, Day 1

What traditions has your family passed down through the generations that are no longer serving you? Your family? Your future family? Think about traditions regarding how relationships are conducted, how affection is expressed (or isn't), how children are disciplined, etc..

_____

_____

_____

_____

_____

_____

_____

_____

Who benefits from keeping those traditions alive? Who benefits if you change them?

_____

_____

_____

_____

_____

_____

_____

_____

_____

_____

If you could create new traditions that are more meaningful for you and your family, what would they be?

_____

_____

_____

_____

_____

_____

_____

_____

_____

_____

_____

Week 7, Day 2

Not all traditions are bad or harmful. Let's take a moment to think about some good things we can carry forward from our past.

Are there traditions in your family that are beneficial to everyone? Is there a way to honor the past while embracing the potential for improvement on the tradition you would like to improve?

_____

_____

_____

_____

_____

_____

_____

_____

_____

Are there any traditions you have witnessed others do that you would love to incorporate into your life and legacy?

_____

_____

_____

_____

_____

_____

_____

_____

_____

_____

_____

Are there new traditions you would like to begin that future generations can look back on as a positive thing?

_____

_____

_____

_____

_____

_____

_____

_____

_____

_____

_____

Week 7, Day 3

Changing traditions is a big step. To prepare for it, let's reflect on some of the small "nos" and "yeses" you have been able to give in recent weeks.

When was the last time you said "no" to something that didn't feel right to you? What happened?

_____

_____

_____

_____

_____

_____

_____

_____

_____

Is there something in your life that you are too scared to say "no" to right now? Think hypothetically: what might happen if you did say "no" to it? What *will* happen when you do?

_____

_____

_____

_____

_____

_____

_____

_____

_____

_____

_____

_____

What kind of support might help you say "no" to things that don't feel right to you? Are there people you could call on for support like that, or plans you could make to obtain that kind of support for yourself

_____

_____

_____

_____

_____

_____

_____

_____

_____

_____

Week 7, Day 4

Today, let's think about saying "yes." What was the last thing you said "yes" to, enthusiastically and wholeheartedly? Why did you say "yes," and how did that feel in your body?

How often do you get to say an enthusiastic and wholehearted "yes?" If it doesn't happen every day, how can you take action to create more situations where you are offered what you really want?

_____

_____

_____

_____

_____

_____

_____

_____

_____

_____

Week 7, Day 5

Now that you have refreshed yourself on what a strong "yes" feels like in your body, I invite you to read back over the previous entries from this week.

What do the traditions you want to change feel like in your body? Might awareness of this "no" in your body help empower you to push for them to change?

_____

_____

_____

_____

_____

_____

_____

_____

_____

What about the traditions that you love, or new traditions you want to create? Do you feel a powerful "yes" on your body when you think of these? Can you use these traditions to give people in your family more opportunities to say an enthusiastic "yes?"

_____

_____

_____

_____

_____

_____

_____

_____

_____

_____

What obstacles do you see to being able to express your true feelings and opinions in your life and family? How might these obstacles be removed, avoided, or overcome?

_____

_____

_____

_____

_____

_____

_____

_____

_____

_____

Week 7, Day 6

Today, choose one holiday celebration or gathering and write how you would like to change this tradition, or create a new one.

How would you like this event to be celebrated? What kind of message would your new tradition send? Why did you choose to change this celebration?

_____

_____

_____

_____

_____

_____

_____

_____

_____

_____

_____

_____

_____

_____

_____

_____

While traditions may be rooted in faith, history, and/or outdated expectations, we are also gifted with the ability to discern their true meaning and impact. When you are comfortable, share these thoughts with your family and maybe even encourage their input on how they think these changes could be put in place.

You don't need to get rid of everything that connects you to your history, but you can improve on your family's traditions together. Be prepared for some pushback as you begin your journey of creating the traditions you would like to have, and give others time and space to experience and explore their feelings on these matters. In this way you can help ensure that you will all create the legacy you would like to leave to future generations.

You got this!

Day 7

Day of Rest

Rest, relax, and do something nice for yourself. You've earned it.

Chapter Eight
Déjà Vu

In my memoir, Chapter 8 is where I attempt suicide for the second time. Although I had been learning to make small changes to create the life I wanted, including moving out of my stepdad's house when he violated my boundaries, I still felt like a failure.

Financial necessities had forced me to drop out of college, so now I, who had once been expected to excel beyond my high school classmates, was a college dropout who couldn't afford to put gas in my car. Watching many of my high school friends go on to start homes and begin working in their careers of choice was particularly frustrating.

I couldn't understand: why couldn't I seem to succeed like they did? Part of it was financial, but another part of it was my untreated trauma and depression. I still had not acknowledged that my childhood trauma was important enough that it might be causing my spirals of low self-esteem and self-sabotage, or that I had any legitimate reason or excuse to fail to meet sky-high expectations.

Around this time, I also met my future husband, Reco. He was another godsend, opening my eyes to new ways of thinking and feeling that I once thought were impossible for me. I didn't realize it right away (if you read my memoir you'll get a good laugh reading about his early attempts to court me), but in the end I was about to get another education about what was possible.

To receive this education, I had to push past some learned discomfort with business, and ultimately with entrepreneurs. Reco and my stepdad were both entrepreneurs, and it took some time for me to realize that they were about as different from each other as two people can be. It was Reco's influence that led me to seriously consider the possibility that I could succeed in the world of business, after feeling incompetent and incapable for so long.

Opening ourselves up to something different and letting down our walls can be an intimidating, but ultimately rewarding journey. You want to protect yourself from further hurt and staying in your comfort zone gives you a sense that you can control something. Your comfort zone is basically a defense mechanism. But these comfort zones can sometimes hold ourselves back from becoming our fullest self.

In this chapter, what made the difference was me allowing myself to let my walls down and also trust myself, my feelings, and my decisions. Letting down your walls is about vulnerability, courage, and learning to trust. I'm curious to hear your thoughts and experiences on this path. Let's dig a little deeper into this topic.

Week 8, Day 1

Vulnerability in relationships means showing our true selves to people. This can be an incredibly healing and validating experience, but it can also be incredibly painful if the people we open up to don't honor our trust.

I have found that learning to live more deeply and more freely involves learning to be vulnerable, even though I was often hurt when I exposed my true feelings and my true self.

What are the biggest fears or anxieties you face when it comes to vulnerability?

_____

_____

_____

_____

_____

_____

_____

_____

Are there people you feel safe being vulnerable with, confiding in, or asking for support? What is it about these people that helps you feel safe with them?

_____

_____

_____

_____

_____

_____

_____

_____

_____

_____

Week 8, Day 2

Do you think that letting down your walls more often would change how you connect with others? If so, how? Be honest and vulnerable here: do you think you would feel more fulfilled and connected, or do you think you would be hurt or rejected if you showed more of your true self more often?

_____

_____

_____

_____

_____

_____

_____

_____

_____

_____

If you are afraid of being vulnerable, are there safe spaces where you might be able to practice this? Think of support groups, church groups, therapists and other places people go specifically to heal their emotional wounds. Would you like to join one of these? Why or why not?

Week 8, Day 3

Can you think of a time that you were vulnerable with someone, and something good happened? What did that feel like in your body?

_____

_____

_____

_____

_____

_____

_____

_____

_____

_____

Is there something in particular that feels difficult for you when it comes to being vulnerable and letting your walls down? What makes it challenging to let go of?

_____

_____

_____

_____

_____

_____

_____

_____

_____

_____

Week 8, Day 4

This journey of letting your walls down is often about learning to accept and embrace your vulnerabilities. What are you discovering about yourself and your needs through this process of trusting yourself more and letting others in?

_____

_____

_____

_____

_____

_____

_____

_____

_____

Week 8, Day 5

What are some of the positive outcomes you've experienced from opening up? How has it changed your relationships or your outlook on life?

_____

_____

_____

_____

_____

_____

_____

_____

_____

_____

Week 8, Day 6

What is one small act of vulnerability you could practice today or tomorrow? How might it impact your relationships or your own well-being? How could this act of vulnerability and connection impact your day in a positive way?

_____

_____

_____

_____

_____

_____

_____

_____

_____

Week 8, Day 7
Day of Rest

You have done some heavy lifting this week. Take a rest. You've earned it. Consider spending these days off with someone you feel safe with.

Remember, vulnerability is not a weakness, but a strength. I've learned through therapy that it takes courage to open up and be authentic.

Through the journey of letting your walls down and allowing yourself to be vulnerable, you have to have self-compassion. Be kind to yourself, and take moments to acknowledge that opening up is a process. There will be setbacks and moments of self-doubt, so celebrate every step forward that you take.

If you feel safe with your support system, I invite you to share your answers to the above questions and your own experiences with letting down your walls with your support system and lean on them. If you don't have a support system to lean on, I suggest sharing these answers with a therapist.

Chapter Nine

Eyes and Ears Wide Open

T wo years after I met Reco, I had the privilege of saying one of the biggest "yeses" of my life. I had already become an important partner in his business team; now I became his wife. In the process I learned that Reco would stick by me through thick and thin, even if someone else on his team decided they didn't want me around.

The process of learning that I had what it took to succeed in business was incredibly empowering. I had been raised to believe that running a business was something only especially gifted and powerful people could do. Now that I was learning to ask the right questions, I was learning that it was a matter of skills anyone could learn. Not some special, innate quality that I lacked.

Now that I felt I could provide for myself financially *and* I had a relationship I could feel secure in, I was able to make the decisions that truly felt right for me. I no longer felt I was dependent on pleasing someone who I depended on for material support, or that I had to make myself as small as possible in order to scrape by. For the first time, I felt I could follow my heart without guilt or fear.

In this chapter, I want us to take time to examine our fears, and how we think about our strengths and weaknesses.

Where are our fears or limiting beliefs, like my idea that I lacked some essential, innate quality needed to be a business leader, holding us back? Are we accurately assessing our strengths and weaknesses?

Week 9, Day 1

What makes you nervous or anxious? What do you avoid doing because it scares you? These could be activities, skills, fears, or interactions.

_____

_____

_____

_____

_____

_____

_____

_____

_____

_____

Are these fears serving you? Do you think your life is better or worse because you avoid these activities?

_____

_____

_____

_____

_____

_____

_____

_____

_____

_____

_____

Are these fears rational? Do they genuinely help keep you safe, or are they holding you back unnecessarily? Would you change them if you could?

_____

_____

_____

_____

_____

_____

_____

_____

_____

_____

_____

Week 9, Day 2

What are your current strengths? What are you especially or unusually good at? When we take time to recognize our strengths, this can remind us what we are capable of and encourage us to move forward.

_____

_____

_____

_____

_____

_____

_____

_____

_____

_____

How might you use these strengths more to contribute to your success? Where might these skills or abilities be especially useful in your business, industry, or career path of choice?

_____

_____

_____

_____

_____

_____

_____

_____

_____

What are your current weaknesses? How might you strengthen your skills, knowledge, or emotional resilience in these areas? When we understand our weaknesses, we can identify areas for growth.

_____

_____

_____

_____

_____

_____

_____

_____

_____

_____

Week 9, Day 3

What limiting beliefs do you have that are holding you back? Do any internal voices tell you, "I can't," "I'm not good enough," "I'm too old to learn," or "I'm too afraid of failing?" List as many of these limiting beliefs as you can.

1. _____

2. _____

3. _____

4. _____

5. _____

6. _____

7. _____

8. _____

9. _____

10. _____

11. _____

12. _____

Now, for each of the beliefs above, ask yourself if this is really true. Is there evidence that this is true, or is there evidence to the contrary? Is the thing you "can't do" a matter of natural talent, or a matter of acquiring knowledge and taking the right steps to grow and succeed? Think critically about whether you are really limited in what you can achieve.

1. This belief is _____

2. This belief is _____

3. This belief is _____

4. This belief is _____

5. This belief is _____

6. This belief is _____

7. This belief is _____

8. This belief is _____

9. This belief is _____

10. This belief is _____

11. This belief is _____

12. This belief is _____

How would your life be if you discarded those limiting beliefs? What would you do if you believed you could succeed at anything you tried. How does the thought of starting this endeavor feel in your body?

Week 9, Day 4

What one thing have you always wanted to do but haven't dared to try? Why haven't you tried it yet?

What are some ways you could try out this thing you've always wanted to do, but have never tried? What are small steps you could take toward doing it?

_____

_____

_____

_____

_____

_____

_____

_____

_____

_____

The last question for today is a challenge: set a timer for 15 minutes and take that one step you wrote down towards doing the thing you have always wanted to do. It doesn't matter if you stick with it or not; just having the experience of trying and seeing what happens will broaden your horizons and make you more open to trying other new things in the future.

Week 9, Day 5

What steps can you take this week to celebrate your strengths and incorporate them more fully into your life? Remember, it doesn't have to cost anything to do this. You don't have to go on a shopping spree. If you have been working hard and sleeping less, your celebration can be sleeping in late on your next day off.

How will you celebrate your strengths this week?

_____

_____

_____

_____

_____

_____

_____

_____

Week 9, Day 6

What resources or learning experiences could help you develop your areas of weakness? What are some small, achievable steps you can take to improve?

_____

_____

_____

_____

_____

_____

_____

_____

_____

_____

Sometimes stepping out means letting go. What outdated perspectives or habits can you let go of to make room for the new ones?

_____

_____

_____

_____

_____

_____

_____

_____

_____

_____

Week 9, Day 7
Day of Rest

You have done a lot of work and reflecting this week! If you'd like, take today to read over what you've written on the previous days this week. How do you feel about what you've written now?

Stepping out of our comfort zone is hard. I know it firsthand. There will be stumbles, moments of doubt, and days when the path ahead seems blurry.

But that's the beauty of the journey, isn't it? It's not about arriving at a *perfect* destination. It's about the courage it takes to keep moving, to learn from each stumble, and to find joy in the unexpected twists.

Remember, our comfort zones are sometimes like cozy cages. In order to see what you can do, what your true potential is, you have to stretch yourself and get uncomfortable. Then you can say, "yes, that was good for me," or, "no, that did not serve me." From there you can make the necessary adjustments.

When we step out of our comfort zone, it's like God is unlocking the door of the cozy cage and whispering, "Fly."

Chapter Ten

Something Old, Something New, Something Borrowed... Something's A Clue

M y wedding was a rite of passage in more ways than one. As Reco and I brought our friends and families together to celebrate, with his support, I found myself having to say "no" to many strong feelings and opinions from people around me in order to say "yes" to what felt right to me.

Those who have been brides may relate to this. While the stereotype is that weddings are all about the bride and groom, too often weddings become fertile ground for everyone in the family and social group to try to compete for social status or project their own wishes and beliefs about how things can be done onto the bride and groom.

In my case, I didn't want alcohol at my wedding; some of my family and friends found this idea ridiculous and objected so hard I was afraid they might sneak alcohol in against my wishes. Another friend's husband was fine with her appearing in my bridal party—as long as she wore a turtleneck under her bridesmaid dress to avoid exposing her collarbone to strange men.

This wedding was an opportunity to remember who was in charge of my life: me. More intensely than ever before, I was able to practice saying "no" so that I could create the reality I wanted for me and my family, instead of the reality other people thought we should have.

Let's examine your current practices around saying "yes" or "no" over the course of the week to come.

Week 10, Day 1

Does saying "yes" often leave you feeling drained, resentful, or obligated? Why do you think you say "yes" to requests that leave you feeling this way? If it feels good, dive deep into this answer.

_____

_____

_____

_____

_____

_____

_____

_____

_____

_____

Week 10, Day 2

Does saying "no" trigger guilt, anxiety, or fear of disapproval? What experiences do you think taught you this response?

_____

_____

_____

_____

_____

_____

_____

_____

_____

_____

Does this fear or guilt response to saying "no" happen with work, family, social circles, or a specific person?

_____

_____

_____

_____

_____

_____

_____

_____

_____

_____

_____

What would you be able to do if you lost this feeling of guilt or fear?

_____

_____

_____

_____

_____

_____

_____

_____

_____

_____

_____

Week 10, Day 3

Think about a time you said "no" to an opportunity (not a demand) recently. Did the "no" arise from a genuine conflict with your values or desires, or was it driven by fear of how others might react if you said "yes?"

_____

_____

_____

_____

_____

_____

_____

_____

_____

_____

What about the last time you said "yes?" Was that driven by a genuine, internal "yes," or by a fear of disappointing others or losing their approval?

_____

_____

_____

_____

_____

_____

_____

_____

_____

_____

_____

Would you have answered either of those questions differently if you had been standing fully in your power at the time? What might have happened if you did answer those questions differently?

_____

_____

_____

_____

_____

_____

_____

_____

_____

Week 10, Day 4

Taking a moment to recognize these emotional cues can help you untangle your internal feelings from outside pressures. Write down the first ones that come to your mind. Do not second guess your thoughts.

What brings me joy and fulfillment? How does this feel in my body?

_____

_____

_____

_____

_____

_____

_____

_____

_____

What aligns with my values? How does it feel in my body when I align with my values?

_____

_____

_____

_____

_____

_____

_____

_____

_____

_____

What are some ways I can experience these feelings more often in my daily life this week?

_____

_____

_____

_____

_____

_____

_____

_____

_____

_____

Week 10, Day 5

Just like yesterday, write down the first thing that comes to mind. Don't second-guess yourself. What matters most to you?

_____

_____

_____

_____

_____

_____

_____

_____

_____

_____

What principles do you want to live by?

_____

_____

_____

_____

_____

_____

_____

_____

_____

_____

_____

_____

_____

_____

_____

_____

_____

_____

_____

_____

_____

_____

_____

This self-awareness helps to clarify your personal priorities and build a foundation for authentic choices.

Week 10, Day 6

Let's complete one exercise my therapist encouraged me to do, which was creating a "filter plan." This filter plan helps you prioritize genuine "yeses" and "nos." It helps you avoid saying "yes" just to please others at your own expense. It also helps you realize that saying "no" isn't about denying others, but about protecting your own well-being and respecting your limitations. Saying "no" empowers you to prioritize your own needs .Before saying "yes" or "no" to anything, ask yourself: "Is this aligned with my values and goals?" "Does it bring me joy or fulfillment?" "Am I able to fully do what I am being asked?" Here are some reminders that might be helpful:

- Saying "no" is a skill that can be learned and strengthened with practice. Start small, with saying "no" to minor requests, and gradually build your confidence. You can say "no" in a nice way.

- Sometimes, instead of simply saying "no," explain your reasons briefly and respectfully. This helps manage expectations and sets healthy boundaries without being hurtful or dismissive. This is called assertive communication.

- Focus on the positive outcomes of assertive communication. Saying "no" opens doors to saying "yes" to opportunities that truly resonate with you and align with your goals.

- Setting boundaries and saying "no" is not selfish, it's an act of self-care. By prioritizing your needs, you create space for genuine connection and avoid depleting your energy.

- Embrace the power of "yes" to your true desires and values. Saying "yes" to experiences that ignite your passion fuels personal growth and unlocks new possibilities. Celebrate these "yeses" as stepping stones on your journey to self-discovery.

- Seek support and encouragement from trusted friends, family, or a therapist. Having a supportive network can help you navigate challenges and celebrate your progress.

Now, let's create your filter plan. I suggest answering these questions on a separate sheet of paper and then writing the final plan on the lines below.

1. Identify your boundaries for the five areas below:

    a. Physical boundaries: personal space, touch, sexual/sensual, privacy

    b. Emotional boundaries: sharing feelings, expressing vulnerability

    c. Mental boundaries: opinions, beliefs, thoughts

    d. Time boundaries: commitments, availability, work-life balance

    e. Material boundaries: possessions, finances, resources

2. Define your filters:

    a. Decide what's acceptable or unacceptable.

    b. Keep in mind and consider your energy level, emotional capacity, and values. Ask what drains you and what encourages you.

3. Identify and write down the different ways that you can say "no".
Use the suggestions from the previous page if you need help.

_____

_____

_____

_____

_____

_____

_____

_____

_____

_____

_____

Now that you have this filter plan, make sure to reinforce your boundaries, stay consistent with upholding them, and know that it is ok to remind others when they cross or violate your boundaries. It is also important (and ok) to distance yourself from those who repeatedly disregard your boundaries.

Remember, boundaries may evolve as you grow and change as you evolve. Seek support from friends, family, or a therapist if needed.

The journey to becoming a confident, self-directed decision maker is a continuous process. Be patient with yourself, learn from your mistakes, and celebrate every step you take towards claiming your voice and living a life true to yourself filled with authenticity, purpose, and fulfillment.

By digging deep into the pros and cons of "yes" and "no," you can unlock a powerful tool for self-discovery and personal growth. I hope these questions and insights help you on this journey, and empower you to navigate the "yeses" and "nos" with confidence, authenticity, and self-compassion.

Week 10, Day 7
Day of Rest

Take time to do something nice for yourself today. If you'd like something to do, you may wish to review your filter plan and be ready to apply it to the choices facing you next week.

Chapter Eleven

Planted, Not Buried

I remember the first time I bought a new car when I finally started making money. I'd spent years driving a car that was older than I was and was just grateful to have a reasonably reliable set of wheels that wasn't visibly falling apart. So when the time came to get a new car, I set my sights low. Too low, according to Reco.

"Now, you don't have to get a luxury car," he told me one day, after he caught me looking at used cars on the Internet. "But at least pick out what model and what color you want."

I looked up at him. "Any Toyota will do," I insisted. "As long as it's newer than that old Honda out there."

"No." He shook his head stubbornly. "You are successful. You get to have *preferences*. What *color* Toyota do you want? What color brings you joy?"

I thought about it. "Blue," I said finally. Both because the color blue is my favorite and because I'd read somewhere it was the least likely color of car to be pulled over by police. My survival instincts were still very much driving my decisions.

Later even that would change. At the time, Reco always had red cars, with shiny rims. Flashy, luxury cars, and a color that attracted cops. I finally drove his luxury car and it was a beautiful drive and would further open my mind to what I could consider possible. Now that things were changing in my life, spiritually, mentally, physically, and financially, I began to believe that maybe I had a *right* to be noticed, to attract attention, without fearing that I was doing something wrong.

The road to becoming Chief Operating Officer made me a more complete woman. I'm not sure if that statement sounds ridiculous or cliche, but it's true.

Becoming successful in business taught me that I was competent beyond my wildest dreams. I didn't need to follow orders or rely on others to tell me what to do to become successful. I *did,* however, need to develop my knowledge and my skills, and be coachable. But this wasn't some mystical achievement that was forever just beyond arms' reach. It was well within reach. It just took the discipline to take responsibility for the consequences of my actions.

Realizing that I was competent began to undo some of that childhood trauma. With all the evidence piling up before my eyes and the work I had put in through therapy, I could no longer deny that I was *powerful*, not in the sense of having power over other people but in the sense of being able to make things happen on my own.

With these changes, I began to understand that I didn't need to be afraid anymore. I did not need to *depend* on anybody's approval, so I didn't have to watch my every move, the way I dressed, or the color of my car.

I could live for me, and the family I had chosen, the family who supported me and helped me step into my power and my worth, instead of holding me back.

Finally. Finally, I was free. I was *seeing* me the way God created me.

***

Setting expectations is key in life, from personal relationships to professional endeavors. Having expectations and standards provides clarity and direction, and prevents misunderstandings. Clear expectations eliminate guesswork and ambiguity. They provide a sense of accountability, motivating everyone to perform to the best of their abilities.

We are often led by social expectations set by others. But what expectations do you have set for yourself and your future? What will you and won't you accept in both your personal and professional lives? Expectations should evolve, just like you. But never lose sight of your core values and desires.

My therapist advised me that my expectations should:

1. Provide directions that guide my decisions and actions towards my desired outcome.

2. Feed my motivation in achieving my goals, keeping me energized and focused, and propelling me in a positive direction when faced with challenges.

3. Enhance resilience because I know I will experience setbacks and they better equip me to handle the setbacks and bounce back stronger and wiser.

4. Shape my reality and expectations, because ultimately they are what influence and shape how I perceive experiences and opportunities and interact with others.

5. Create accountability by setting standards for myself and holding myself accountable for my personal growth and self-mastery.

Let's begin creating your own expectations. Create expectations that don't limit, but liberate you on your journey and fuel your potential. Answer these questions:

Setting expectations is key in life, from personal relationships to professional endeavors. Having expectations and standards provides clarity and direction, and prevents misunderstandings. Clear expectations eliminate guesswork and ambiguity. They provide a sense of accountability, motivating everyone to perform to the best of their abilities.

We are often led by social expectations set by others. But what expectations do you have for yourself and your future? What will you accept and won't accept in both your personal and professional lives? Expectations should evolve, just like you. But never lose sight of your core values and desires.

Week 11, Day 1

As we begin formulating your expectations for your future, I want to revisit some of the questions we asked at the beginning of this book. It will be interesting to see if your answers have changed in the last 11 weeks.

What are your core values? Identifying your core values sets the foundation for your expectations. What are the principles that guide your life? What matters most to you?

_____

_____

_____

_____

_____

_____

_____

_____

_____

What are your dreams, goals, and desires? Dream BIG and then figure out what is necessary to achieve it. What's the ideal career, relationship, or lifestyle you desire?

_____

_____

_____

_____

_____

_____

_____

_____

_____

_____

Take a moment to read back over your answers in Chapter 1, and see if there have been any changes from when you initially answered the questions. Did writing down your answers feel different this time?

_____

_____

_____

_____

_____

_____

_____

_____

_____

_____

_____

Week 11, Day 2

As we practice setting expectations according to those five criteria, what goal or area of your life would you like the first expectation we create to be focused on? What in your life feels most urgent or important, and most in need of change right now?

_____

_____

_____

_____

_____

_____

_____

_____

_____

_____

_____

What direction do you need to move in this area of life? What are some expectations of yourself, and of the treatment you will tolerate, that can move you in that direction? Consider both expectations about what you will take action to seek out, and expectations about what situations you will leave rather than tolerating if they arise.

_____

_____

_____

_____

_____

_____

_____

_____

_____

_____

_____

_____

How does it feel to consider implementing expectations like these? Does it feel exciting? Scary? Both?

_____

_____

_____

_____

_____

_____

_____

_____

_____

_____

Week 11, Day 3

Read back over the expectations you formulated yesterday. Today, let's apply the next part of the filter to those expectations. Which of the expectations you formulated yesterday feed your motivation and make you feel energized and focused? Which make you want to propel yourself in a positive direction?

_____

_____

_____

_____

_____

_____

_____

_____

How might you tweak these expectations from yesterday to make them more motivating and energizing? How might these expectations be worded to more effectively keep you focused?

_____

_____

_____

_____

_____

_____

_____

_____

_____

_____

Which of these expectations do you feel enhance your resilience? Since you know you will experience setbacks, which of these expectations will enable you to handle these with grace and bounce back stronger and wiser?

_____

_____

_____

_____

_____

_____

_____

_____

_____

_____

_____

Week 11, Day 4

Read back over the expectations you created yesterday? How does it feel to read them now that you've had time to sleep on it? Do they feel expansive and energizing, or restrictive and limiting?

_____

_____

_____

_____

_____

_____

_____

_____

_____

_____

Take a moment to consider how you might revise these expectations to feel more expansive and less restrictive. How can you formulate them to invite more of the possibilities you want without allowing for the possibilities you want to get rid of?

_____

_____

_____

_____

_____

_____

_____

_____

_____

_____

_____

Looking at the expectations you have written down now, how will these shape your reality if you implement them in your life? How might they change your experiences and your worldview if you stick to enforcing them?

_____

_____

_____

_____

_____

_____

_____

_____

_____

_____

Week 11, Day 5

What expectations or goals can you set to create accountability for yourself? Accountability means taking responsibility for both the good and bad things in your life. As adults we are able to take responsibility for where we choose to stay, who we choose to stay with, what kind of treatment of ourselves we choose to tolerate, etc., as well as how we use our time to nurture ourselves and work toward our goals.

What are some accountability standards you can set for yourself based on the expectations you've developed over the last few days? What are some ways you can hold yourself accountable for choosing growth, leaving bad situations, nourishing yourself, and working toward your goals?

_____

_____

_____

_____

_____

_____

_____

_____

One of the most challenging and nuanced parts of personal growth is learning to balance holding yourself accountable with accepting setbacks as a natural part of the growth process. How can you know you are being too hard on yourself? What is a sign you may need to push a little harder to reach your goals?

_____

_____

_____

_____

_____

_____

_____

_____

_____

_____

_____

_____

_____

_____

_____

_____

_____

_____

_____

_____

_____

If something feels off, don't be afraid to adjust or even let go. Your intuition is a powerful guide.

Week 11, Days 6 & 7
Days of Rest

Take these days to rest and reflect on what you've learned in these last few chapters. And celebrate your victory in nearing the completion of this journey!

Chapter Twelve

Closed Door, Opened Window

I n the last chapter of my memoir, I learn that I am pregnant against all odds—only to miscarry a few weeks after finding out. My miscarriage would start me on the path to attending therapy with my husband and ultimately to opening up on social media about my grief for my lost child.

To my astonishment, my opening up would lead to an outpouring of support—and of other women telling me how supported *they* felt upon hearing my story, having previously believed they were alone in their own pain.

From then on, I resolved that this would be part of my mission. If sharing my own trauma could help others to feel less alone in theirs, then it was something I had to do.

I want to close this journal by offering a meditation exercise.

Meditation is the practice of taking moments to gather peace, focusing and training the mind to achieve a state of increased awareness, calm, and emotional stability. It helps to detach one's identity from distracting thoughts and emotions. This is shown to be one of the most powerful practices there is for mental health and emotional resilience.

There are many forms of meditation but my favorite is called *Mantra Meditation*. This is when you repeat a specific word or phrase to quiet your mind, often with peaceful and relaxing music playing. This can pair well with affirmations, using affirmations as your mantra.

Below is a guided meditation. I suggest you record yourself reading the meditation and then play it for yourself when you need it. Find moments to meditate. I meditate before bed, after exercising, when my anxiety increases, and when I just need to have a moment of peace.

Affirmations for Meditation:

1. My mistakes are stepping stones to my success.

2. I am worthy of love, respect, and happiness.

3. I radiate positive energy and attract like-minded people.

4. I celebrate my victories, big and small.

5. I am grateful for the journey of personal growth, even the stumbles and setbacks.

6. I release negativity and embrace the joy of being alive.

7. I am learning to love and accept myself, flaws and all.

8. I forgive others and let go of resentment.

9. I embrace that difficulties are temporary, but my growth is permanent.

10. I release doubt and fear, knowing God's plan for me is greater than

my understanding.

11. God's blessings flow freely into my life, and I welcome them with open arms.

12. I was made in God's image and I am worthy of God's abundance in my life.

Now, create some affirmations of your own:

1.

2.

3.

4.

5.

Meditation

Find a comfortable position: You can sit cross-legged (or as some people say, "criss cross applesauce"), on a chair with your feet flat on the floor, or even lie down if you prefer. Make sure your spine is straight and your body is relaxed.

Close your eyes or soften your gaze: Allow your focus to turn inward, away from external distractions.

Begin with your breath: Breathe in and in your head count to five slowly. Now hold your breath and count to four slowly. Finally, blow out your breath and count to five slowly. Notice the gentle rise and fall of your chest.

Feel the cool air as you inhale and the warmth as you exhale. Don't try to control your breath, simply observe its natural rhythm.

Focus on your body: Scan your body from head to toe, paying attention to any sensations you experience. Notice any areas of tension or tightness, and focus on relaxing those areas. Notice how when you breathe out those begin to relax more and more.

Imagine a peaceful place: Think of a place that brings you a sense of peace and tranquility. It could be a real place you've visited, a dream landscape, or even simply a serene state of mind. Immerse yourself in the details: the sights, sounds, smells, and textures. Feel the calmness of this place surrounding you.

Let go of thoughts and worries: As thoughts arise, acknowledge them without judgment and then gently let them go, like clouds drifting across the sky. Don't get caught up in their stories, simply return your attention to your breath and your peaceful place.

Repeat a calming mantra: Repeat a calming mantra or phrase silently to yourself. If you want to say it out loud, make sure it is just slightly over a whisper. Some examples include: "I am calm," "I am at peace," "I breathe in peace, I breathe out stress," or "Let go and let be."

Stay in this state of calmness for as long as you like: There is no right or wrong amount of time for this meditation. Simply enjoy the feeling of serenity and stillness. Mediations can last for 5 minutes or 15 minutes.

Gently come out of the meditation: When you feel ready, take a few deep breaths

and slowly bring your awareness back to your surroundings. Open your eyes, if you closed them, and wiggle your fingers and toes. Carry the feeling of peace with you throughout your day.

I challenge you to continue this meditation practice every day after completing your 12th week with this journal. Even if it is only for five minutes a day, practice this meditation and then record your thoughts afterwards.

Now might be a good time to obtain a new journal and try making up your own journal prompts, seeking out the questions you need to continue on your journey of growth and healing.

Most of us start our adult lives with some kind of trauma in our past. Many of us start out feeling unworthy, or "not good enough."

The reasons for that are many. It can be the survival skills our families learned in the bad "good" old days or the injustices of the modern day. It can be people who actually meant harm, or people who wanted to help but didn't know how.

The important thing is, we are all here together. And we are all learning our own lessons all the time. For me, part of my calling is to teach mine—to teach what I have learned from experience, in the hope that it might save somebody some time. Or just help somebody feel seen in the darkness of a life where they're afraid to step into the light.

My message in this book is that it's okay to choose yourself. Many of us are taught that it's *not* okay to set boundaries or have needs. Many of us have been taught that we are worthy only when we are obeying or serving others.

And there's the trick of it. Because "serving others" *is* fulfilling. But "serving others" doesn't just mean doing whatever you're told. Sometimes what "others" need is to be told "no." Sometimes what the world needs is for *certain* people to be told "no," so that we can find our larger purpose.

I would not have been able to serve the way I'm serving now if I had done what I was told when I was younger. I would not have learned these skills, or come into my power, or seen the needs nobody was addressing if I had followed the path that was laid out for me. I wouldn't be able to share my story, or stand before you today, if I was too afraid of hurting someone's feelings to speak my truth.

In other words, I wouldn't be able to serve you now if I had not first chosen myself, chosen to do what *I* needed and what *I* thought was right.

Life is not a straight line. It is filled with valleys and victories. We're going to stumble, we're going to make some bad choices, and some of us will carry scars that run deep from pain and loss. The lie that we have been told and taught is that time heals all wounds. The truth is, time cannot heal all wounds nor can it erase them. The healing comes from changing how we view things, our mindset, our willingness to take the steps to dig deep and get to the root of it all.

Yes, the past whispers in our ears and reminds us of what happened, but it does not have to define us or our purpose. Our pain, though real and valid, does not have to dictate our promise. The people who may have wronged us or hurt us do not hold the key to our passion.

I have been through a lot, and I know without any doubt, there are many people who have gone through much, much more than I have. I am sure they too have wanted to give up when times got so rough. My tough times have allowed me to appreciate the great times and to also give me moments to pat myself on the back for my resilience, growth, and perseverance.

I am proud of the woman I have become. I know I have more room to grow and evolve and look forward to doing just that. I know I will have moments of regression, doubt, and self-sabotage because I am human, I am a work in progress, and I have been through high highs and low lows. The important thing is to bounce back and have people in my life that will help catch me when I fall and encourage me to get back up. But it has to be ME and MY decision to do so.

Despite it all, I believe God has given us a pen to rewrite the story of our lives. He gave us a pen, not a pencil, so we won't focus or waste time trying to go back and erase the past, the lessons that come with it, or the setbacks, disappointments, or unmet goals. What we can do is turn the page and begin a new chapter. Leave the old chapters there because they hold lessons, scars that tell stories of strength and resilience while evolving.

If I could leave you with these as final thoughts. The setback may not be your fault, but the comeback is your responsibility. So unleash the power within to go after your God-given purpose. And, remember, God makes no mistakes.

That includes you.

About the Author

Shaneé McCambry is a proud mother of three, business owner, and women's empowerment advocate. She resides with her husband, Reco McCambry, her children Reco Jr., Raegan, and Rylee, and always acknowledges her one child up in Heaven. She is a graduate of Georgia Southern University and was a former Middle Grades Educator for 5 years.

She currently serves as the Chief Operating Officer for Novae. As a female business leader, she is a part of the International Association of Women, 100 Women In Finance, and Dell Women's Entrepreneur Network. She has been featured in Yahoo! Finance, Black Enterprise, VoyageATL, Who's Who In Black Atlanta, and more.

Shaneé is passionate about empowering and uplifting women and has been frequently tapped for speaking engagements for women empowerment as well as hosting her own 2 day women's empowerment conference, Women That Win. Building others up is one her greatest passions and loves inspiring others to see their own greatness, strengths, potential, and growth. She is intentional about sharing her continual journey of working on herself, finding ways to love all of her perfect imperfections, her faith, and genuinely wanting to make sure that she is a light in the lives of those she comes into contact with.

When she's not running her business or being a mother to her children, she loves DIY projects, and she's drawn to the ocean and finds solace and serenity in the sound and vision of the waves. She loves to travel the world and tries not to let her picky eating interfere with her love of learning about new cultures.

www.ingramcontent.com/pod-product-compliance
Lightning Source LLC
Chambersburg PA
CBHW071154130626

46553CB00004B/1656